GRAPHIC LIBRARY™

GRAPHIC SCIENCE

THE EARTH-SHAKING FACTS ABOUT EARTHQUAKES

WITH

MAX AXIOM™ SUPER SCIENTIST

4D An Augmented Reading Science Experience

by Katherine Krohn | illustrated by Tod Smith and Al Milgrom

Consultant:
Professor Kenneth H. Rubin
Department of Geology and Geophysics
School of Ocean and Earth Science and Technology
University of Hawaii, Honolulu

CAPSTONE PRESS
a capstone imprint

T0051016

Graphic Library is published by Capstone Press,
1710 Roe Crest Drive, North Mankato, Minnesota 56003.
www.mycapstone.com

Library of Congress Cataloging-in-Publication Data is available on the Library of Congress website.

ISBN: 978-1-5435-5871-5 (library binding)
ISBN: 978-1-5435-6004-6 (paperback)
ISBN: 978-1-5435-5881-4 (eBook PDF)

Summary: In graphic novel format, follows the adventures of Max Axiom as he explains the science behind earthquakes.

Art Director and Designer
Bob Lentz

Colorist
Krista Ward

Media Researcher
Jo Miller

Cover Artist
Tod Smith

Editor
Christine Peterson

Photo Credits
Capstone Studio: Karon Dubke, 29, back cover; Shutterstock: untitled (map)

Printed in the United States 5685

TABLE OF CONTENTS

SECTION 1

SHAKY GROUND 4

SECTION 2

SEISMIC ACTIVITY..................... 10

SECTION 3

SHOCKS AND QUAKES 16

SECTION 4

BEING PREPARED...................... 24

More About Earthquakes 28
Earth-Pounding P-Waves 29
Discussion Questions, Writing Prompts, Take a Quiz!........... 30
Glossary 31
Read More, Internet Sites, Index 32

SECTION 1 SHAKY GROUND

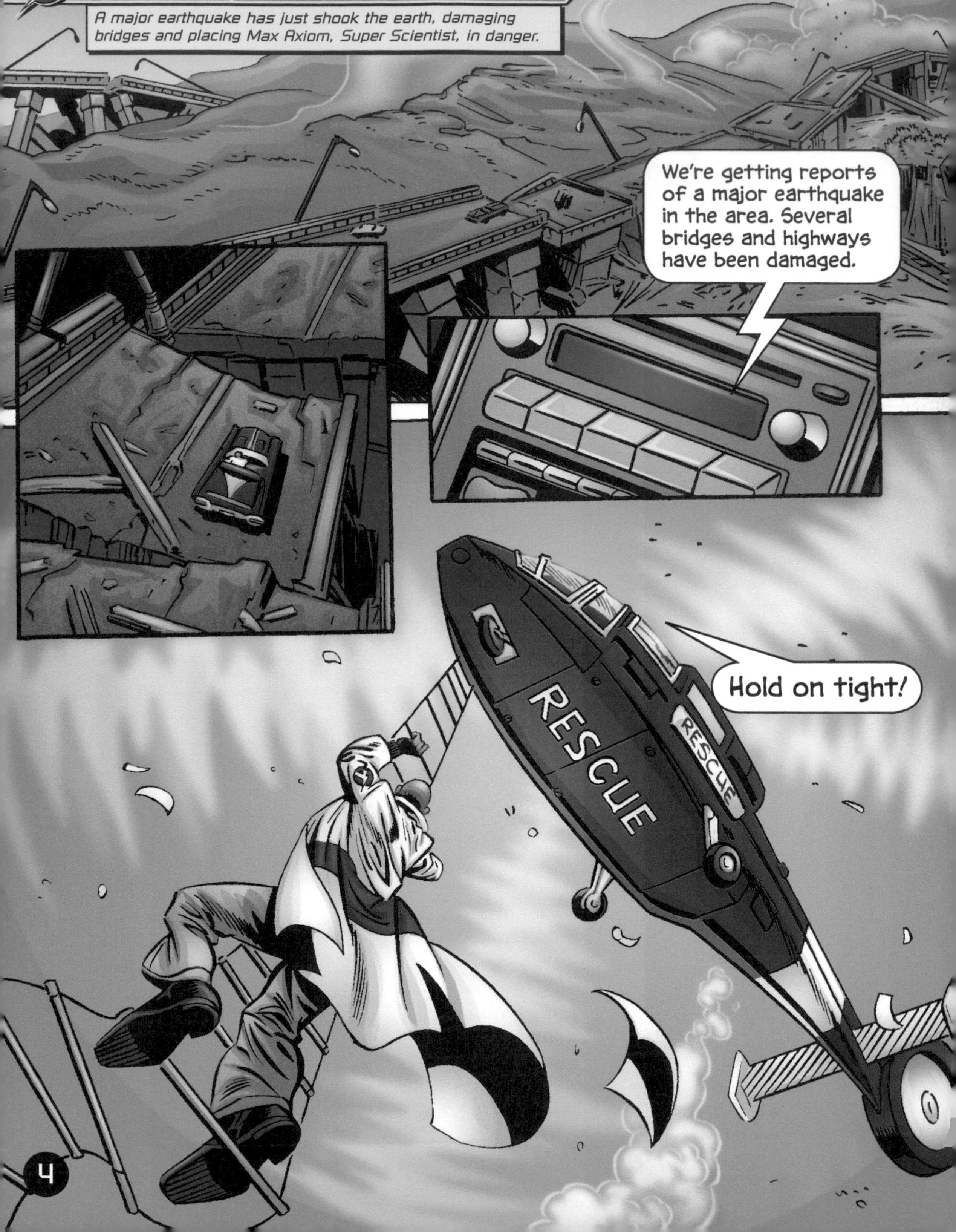
A major earthquake has just shook the earth, damaging bridges and placing Max Axiom, Super Scientist, in danger.
We're getting reports of a major earthquake in the area. Several bridges and highways have been damaged.
Hold on tight!
RESCUE
RESCUE

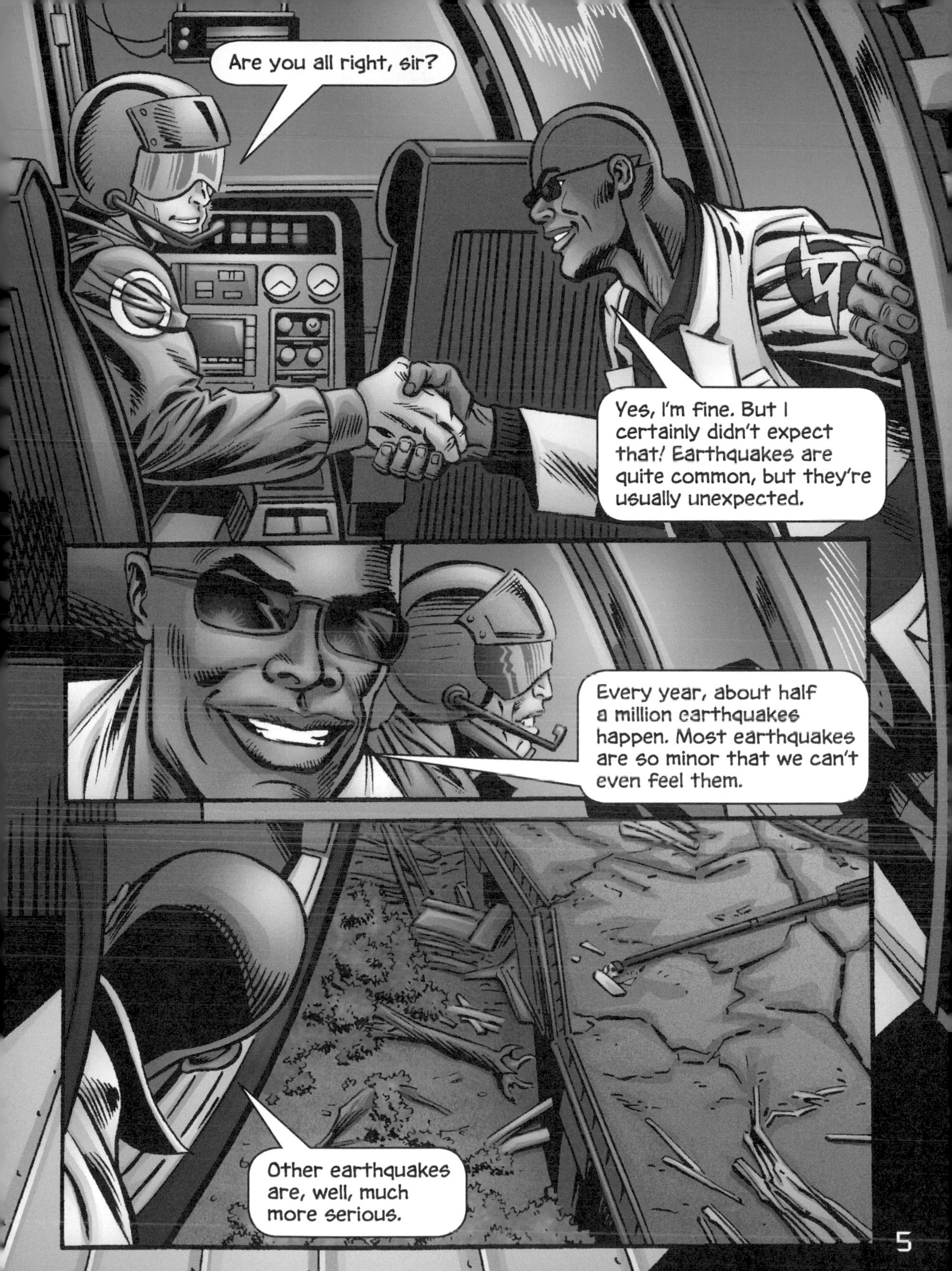
Are you all right, sir?
Yes, I'm fine. But I certainly didn't expect that! Earthquakes are quite common, but they're usually unexpected.
Every year, about half a million earthquakes happen. Most earthquakes are so minor that we can't even feel them.
Other earthquakes are, well, much more serious.

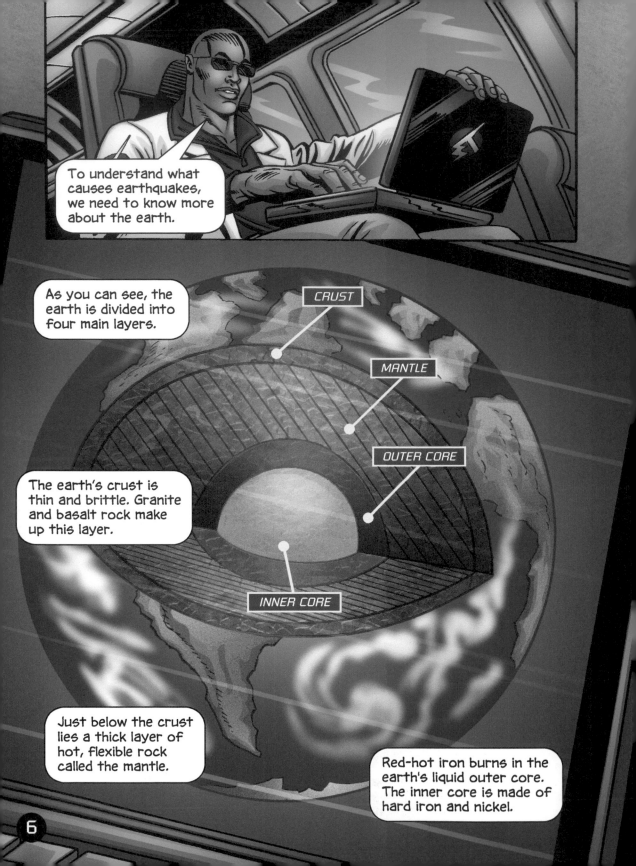

To understand what causes earthquakes, we need to know more about the earth.

As you can see, the earth is divided into four main layers.

CRUST

MANTLE

OUTER CORE

The earth's crust is thin and brittle. Granite and basalt rock make up this layer.

INNER CORE

Just below the crust lies a thick layer of hot, flexible rock called the mantle.

Red-hot iron burns in the earth's liquid outer core. The inner core is made of hard iron and nickel.

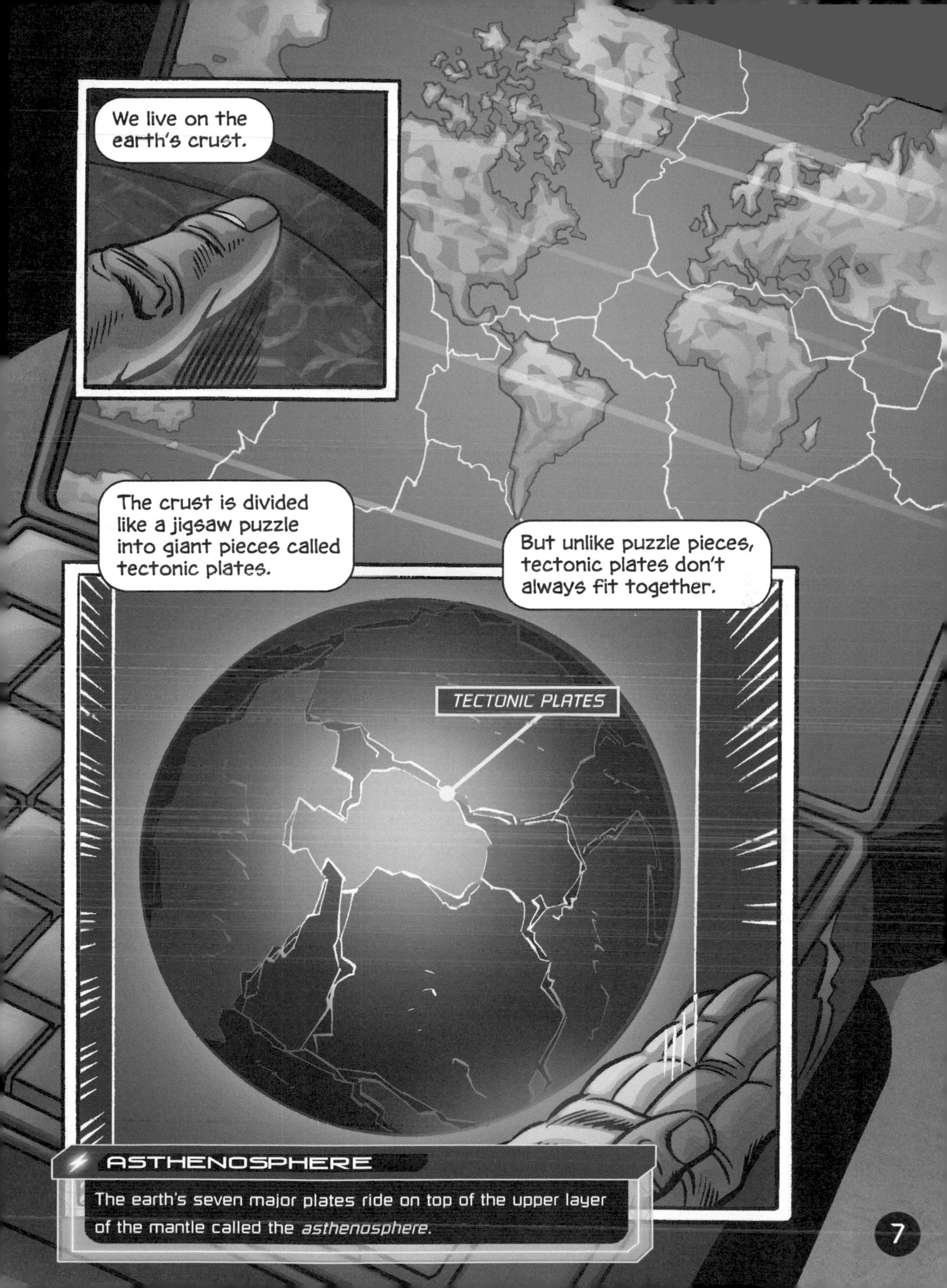
We live on the earth's crust.
The crust is divided like a jigsaw puzzle into giant pieces called tectonic plates.
But unlike puzzle pieces, tectonic plates don't always fit together.
TECTONIC PLATES

ASTHENOSPHERE

The earth's seven major plates ride on top of the upper layer of the mantle called the *asthenosphere*.

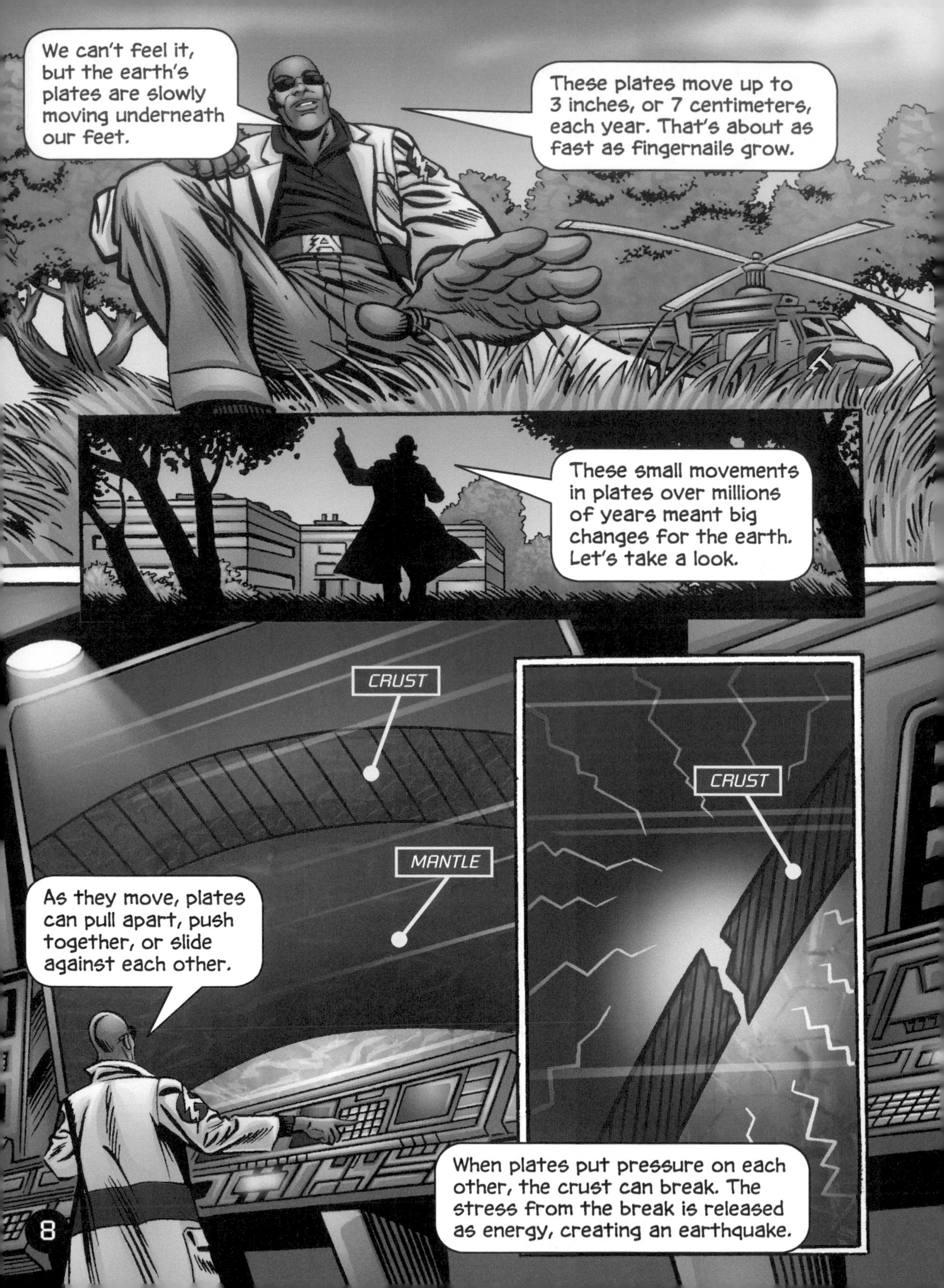
We can't feel it, but the earth's plates are slowly moving underneath our feet.
These plates move up to 3 inches, or 7 centimeters, each year. That's about as fast as fingernails grow.
These small movements in plates over millions of years meant big changes for the earth. Let's take a look.
CRUST
MANTLE
As they move, plates can pull apart, push together, or slide against each other.
CRUST
When plates put pressure on each other, the crust can break. The stress from the break is released as energy, creating an earthquake.

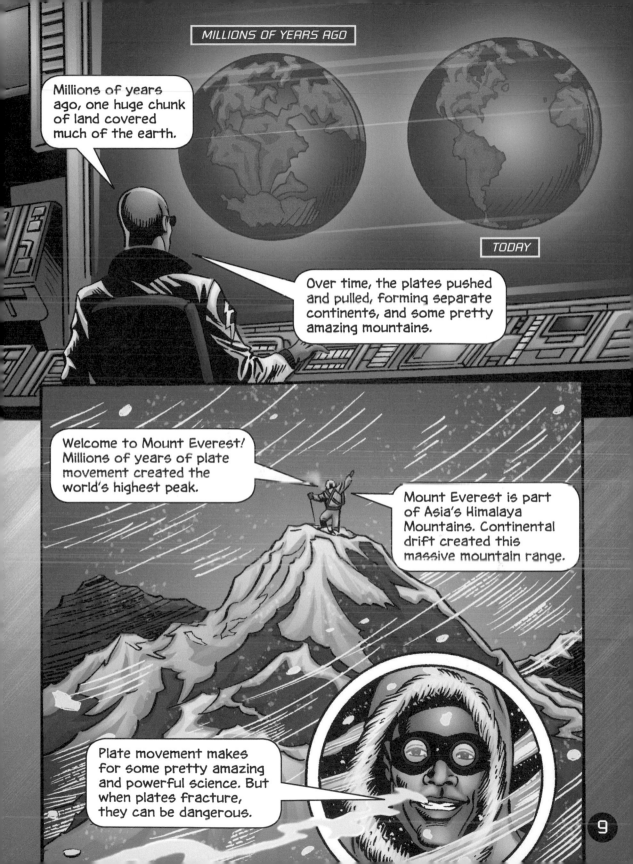

MILLIONS OF YEARS AGO

Millions of years ago, one huge chunk of land covered much of the earth.

TODAY

Over time, the plates pushed and pulled, forming separate continents, and some pretty amazing mountains.

Welcome to Mount Everest! Millions of years of plate movement created the world's highest peak.

Mount Everest is part of Asia's Himalaya Mountains. Continental drift created this massive mountain range.

Plate movement makes for some pretty amazing and powerful science. But when plates fracture, they can be dangerous.

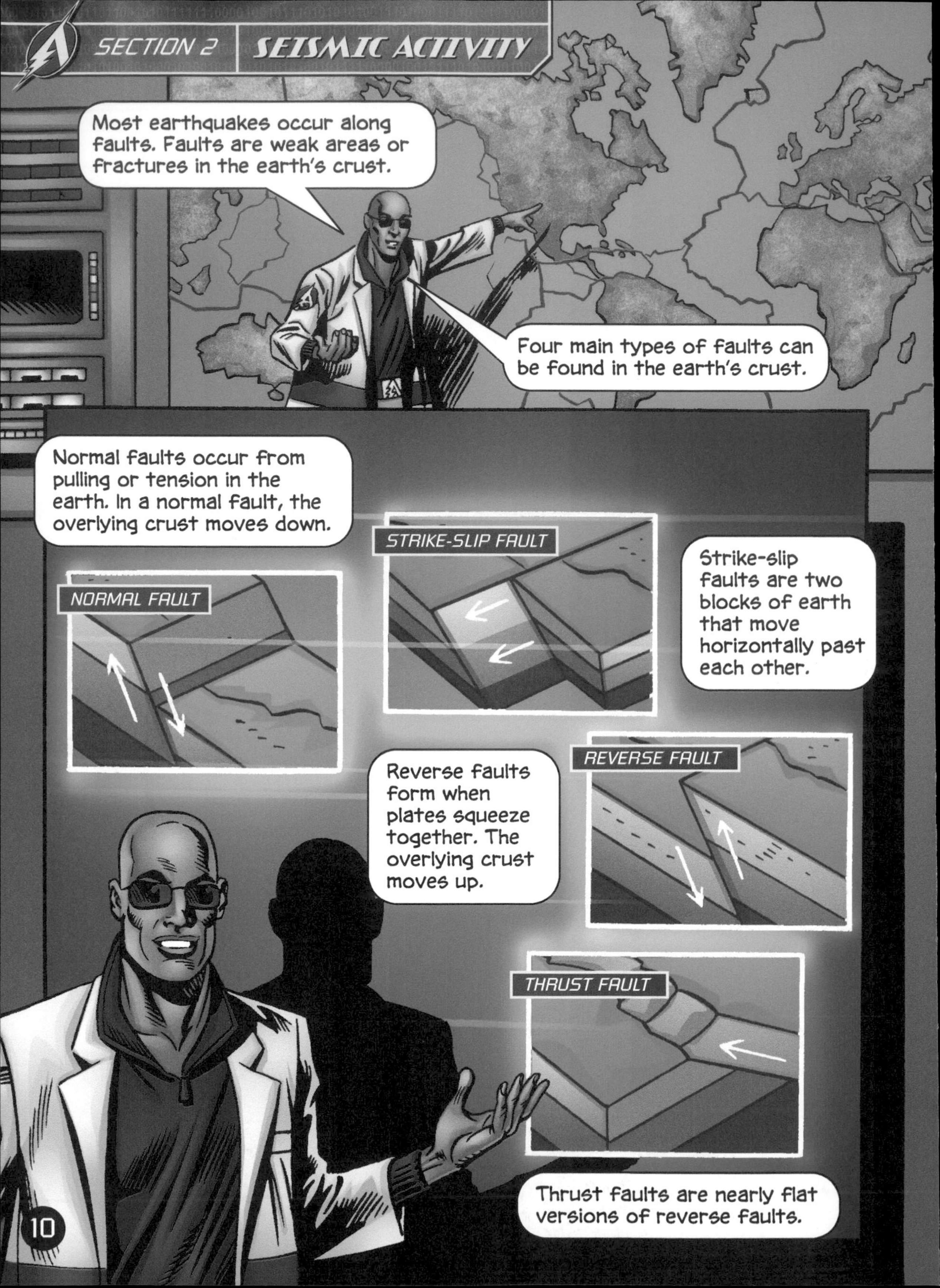
Most earthquakes occur along faults. Faults are weak areas or fractures in the earth's crust.
Four main types of faults can be found in the earth's crust.
Normal faults occur from pulling or tension in the earth. In a normal fault, the overlying crust moves down.
NORMAL FAULT
STRIKE-SLIP FAULT
Strike-slip faults are two blocks of earth that move horizontally past each other.
Reverse faults form when plates squeeze together. The overlying crust moves up.
REVERSE FAULT
THRUST FAULT
Thrust faults are nearly flat versions of reverse faults.

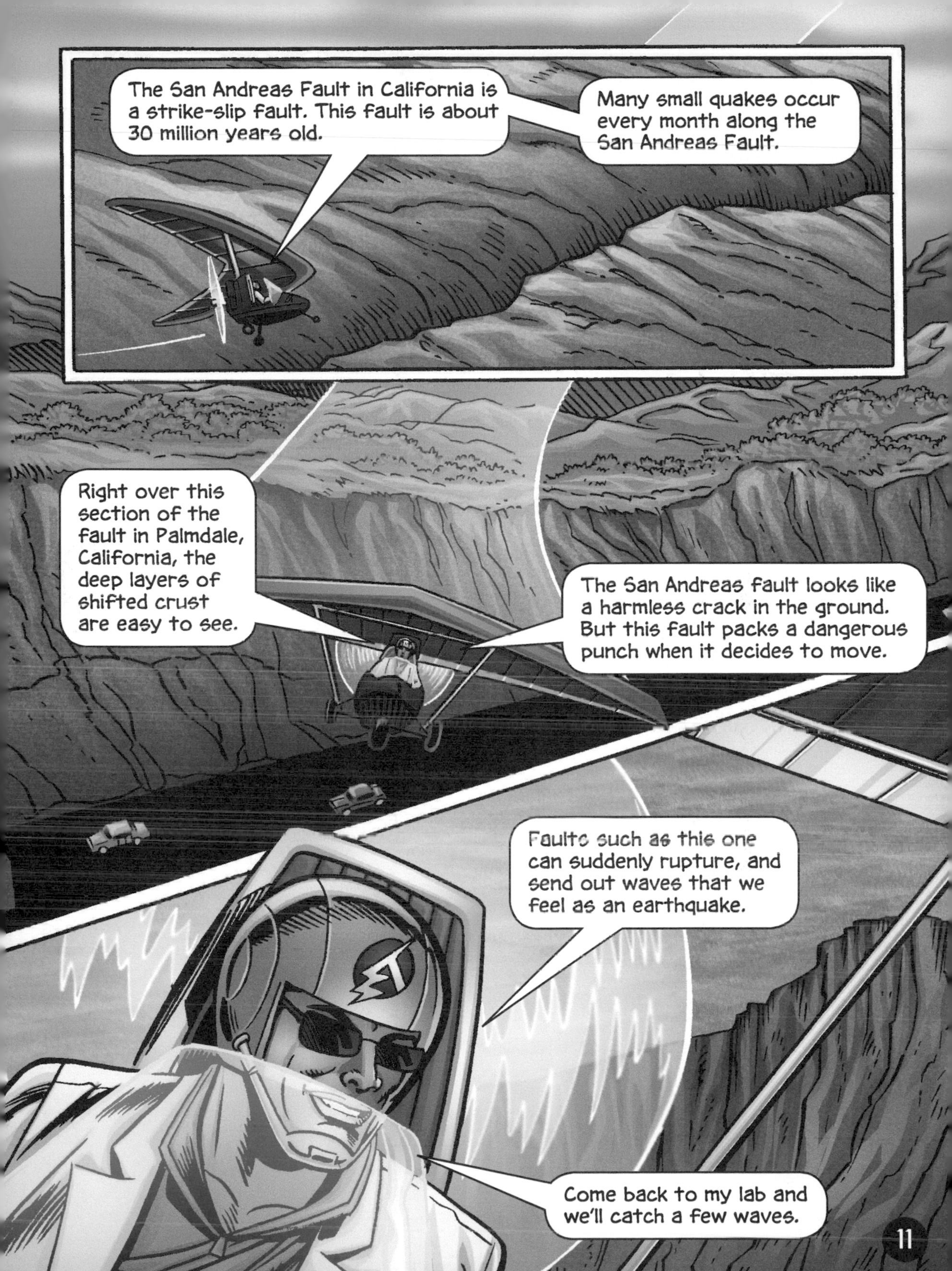
The San Andreas Fault in California is a strike-slip fault. This fault is about 30 million years old.
Many small quakes occur every month along the San Andreas Fault.
Right over this section of the fault in Palmdale, California, the deep layers of shifted crust are easy to see.
The San Andreas fault looks like a harmless crack in the ground. But this fault packs a dangerous punch when it decides to move.
Faults such as this one can suddenly rupture, and send out waves that we feel as an earthquake.
Come back to my lab and we'll catch a few waves.

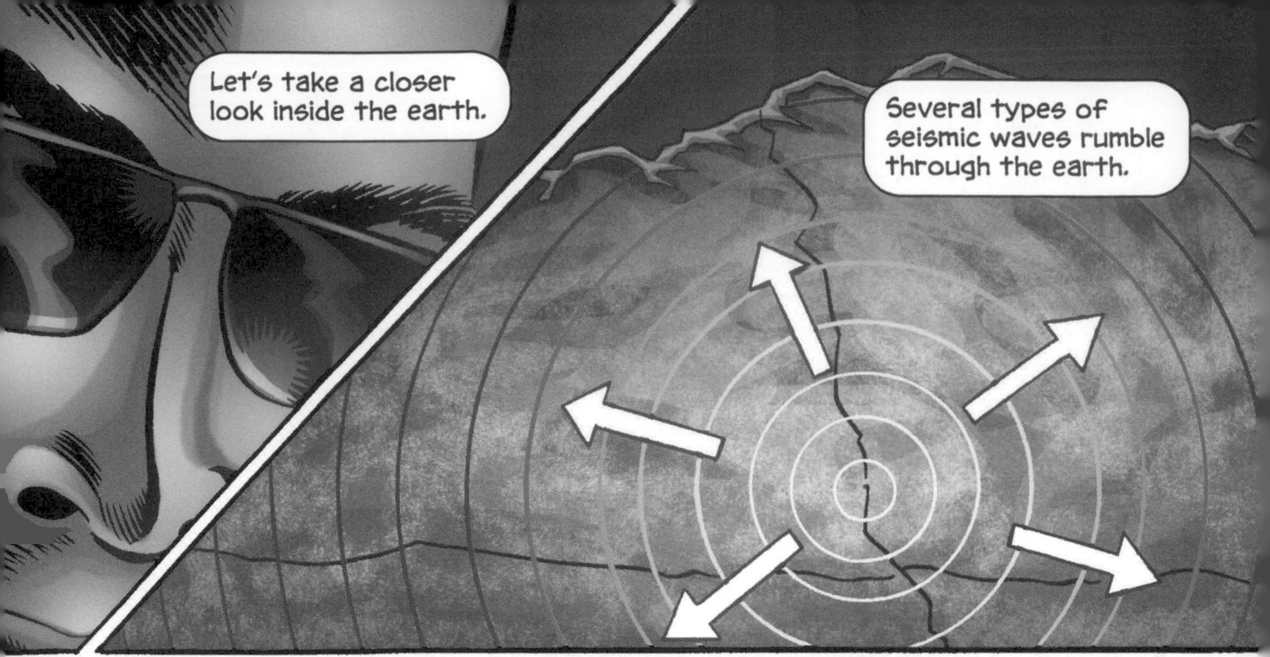
Let's take a closer look inside the earth.
Several types of seismic waves rumble through the earth.

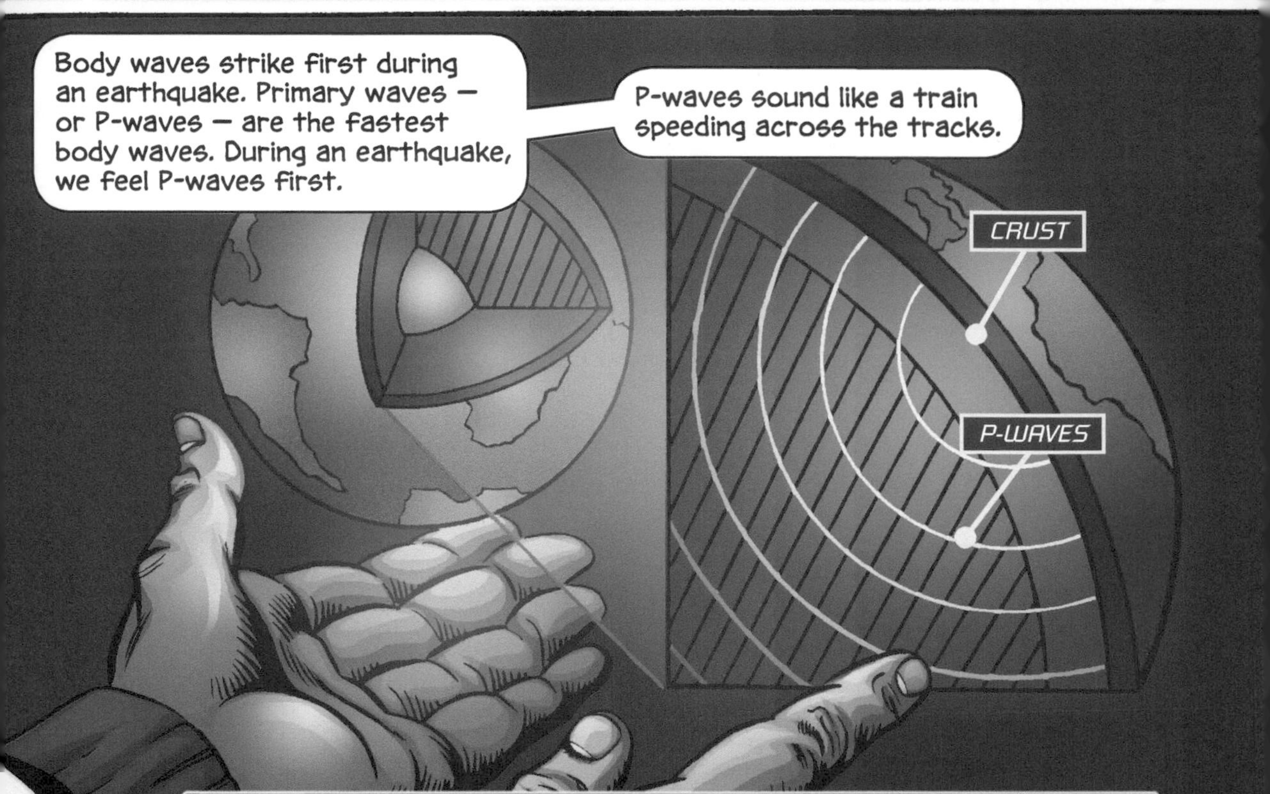
Body waves strike first during an earthquake. Primary waves — or P-waves — are the fastest body waves. During an earthquake, we feel P-waves first.
P-waves sound like a train speeding across the tracks.
CRUST
P-WAVES

QUAKES DEFINED

The focus, or *hypocenter* of an earthquake, is the place in the earth where the earthquake originated. The *epicenter* of an earthquake is the point on the earth's surface directly above the hypocenter.

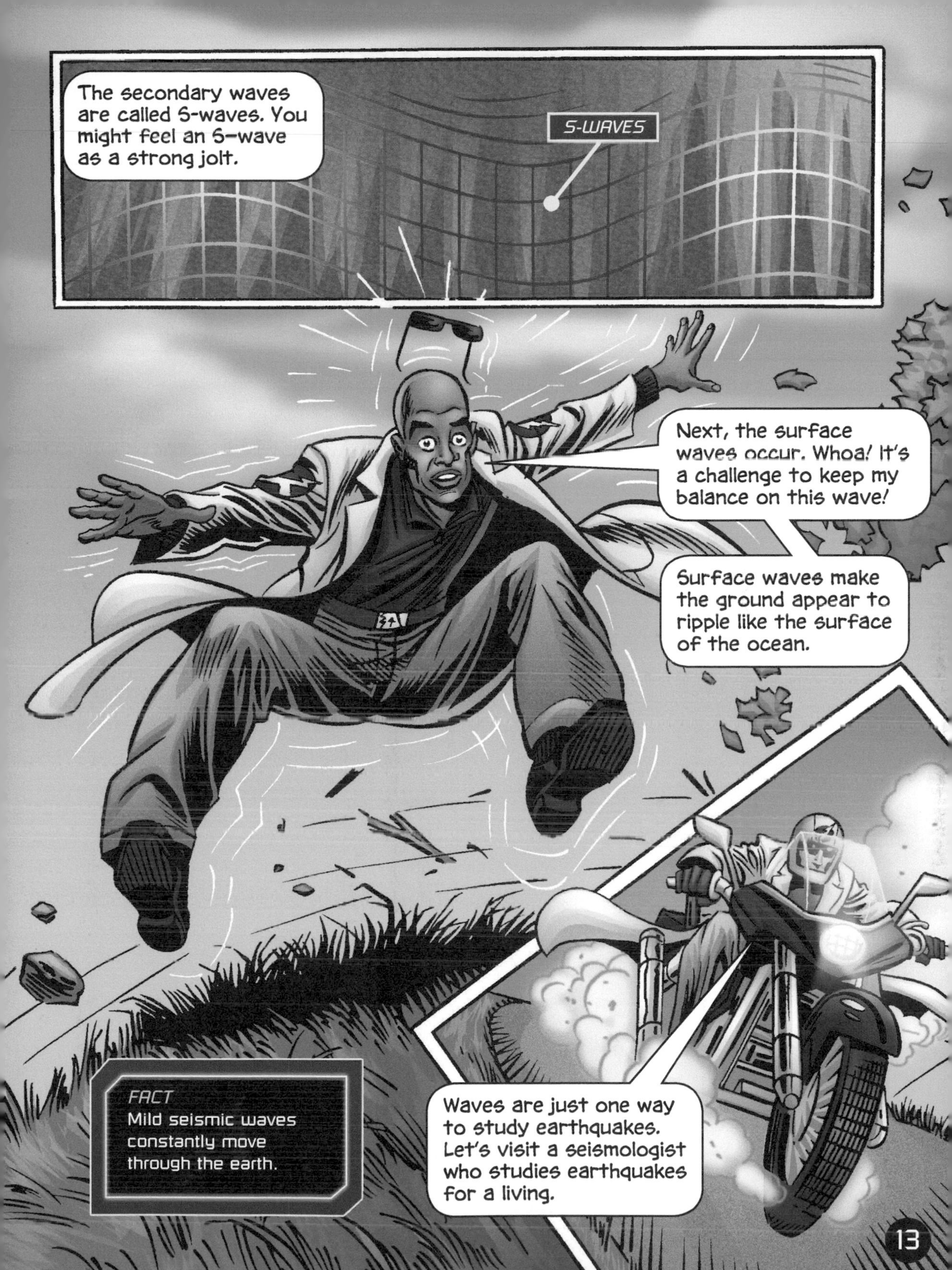
The secondary waves are called S-waves. You might feel an S-wave as a strong jolt.
S-WAVES
Next, the surface waves occur. Whoa! It's a challenge to keep my balance on this wave!
Surface waves make the ground appear to ripple like the surface of the ocean.
FACT
Mild seismic waves constantly move through the earth.
Waves are just one way to study earthquakes. Let's visit a seismologist who studies earthquakes for a living.

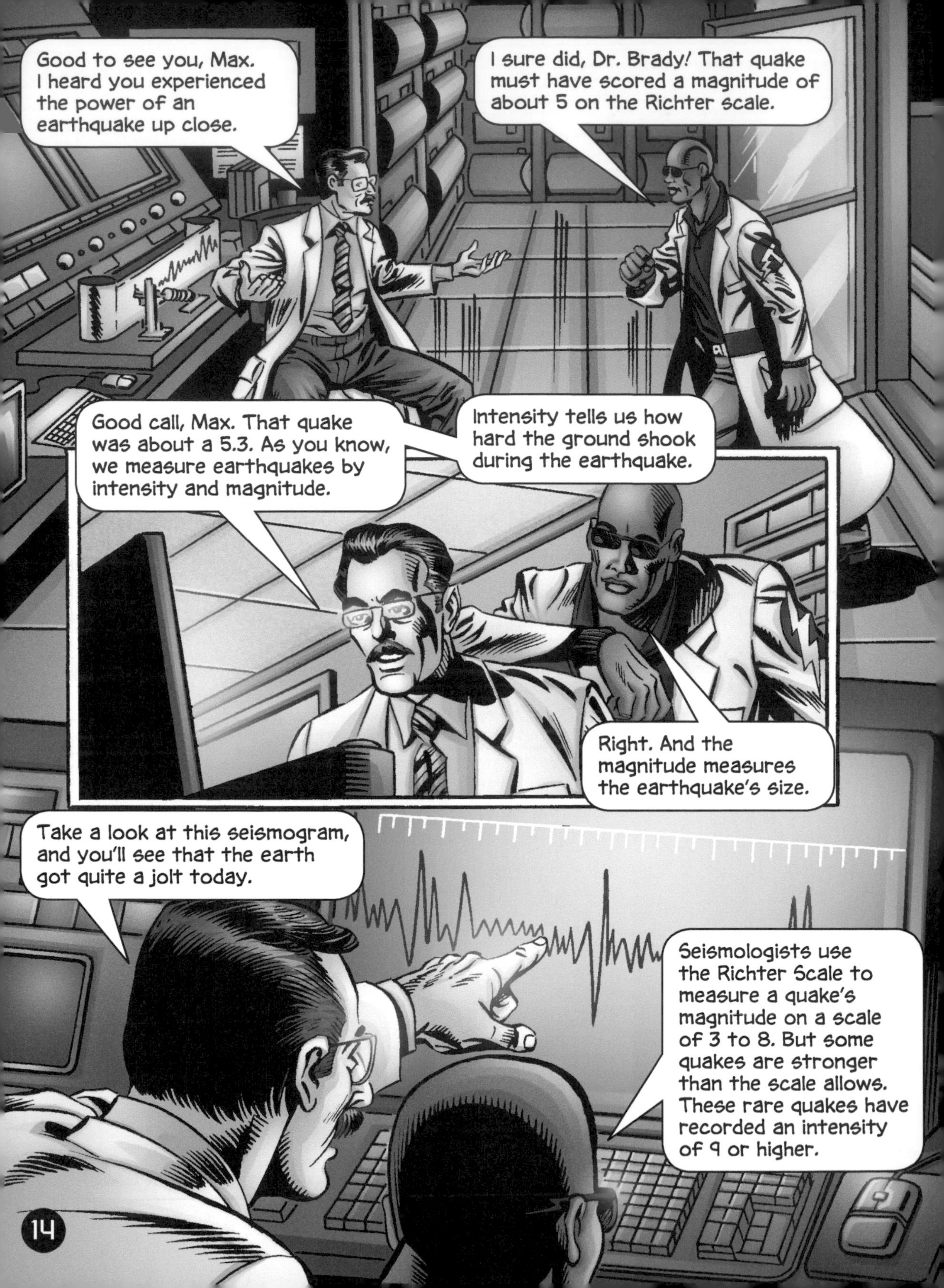
Good to see you, Max. I heard you experienced the power of an earthquake up close.
I sure did, Dr. Brady! That quake must have scored a magnitude of about 5 on the Richter scale.
Good call, Max. That quake was about a 5.3. As you know, we measure earthquakes by intensity and magnitude.
Intensity tells us how hard the ground shook during the earthquake.
Right. And the magnitude measures the earthquake's size.
Take a look at this seismogram, and you'll see that the earth got quite a jolt today.
Seismologists use the Richter Scale to measure a quake's magnitude on a scale of 3 to 8. But some quakes are stronger than the scale allows. These rare quakes have recorded an intensity of 9 or higher.

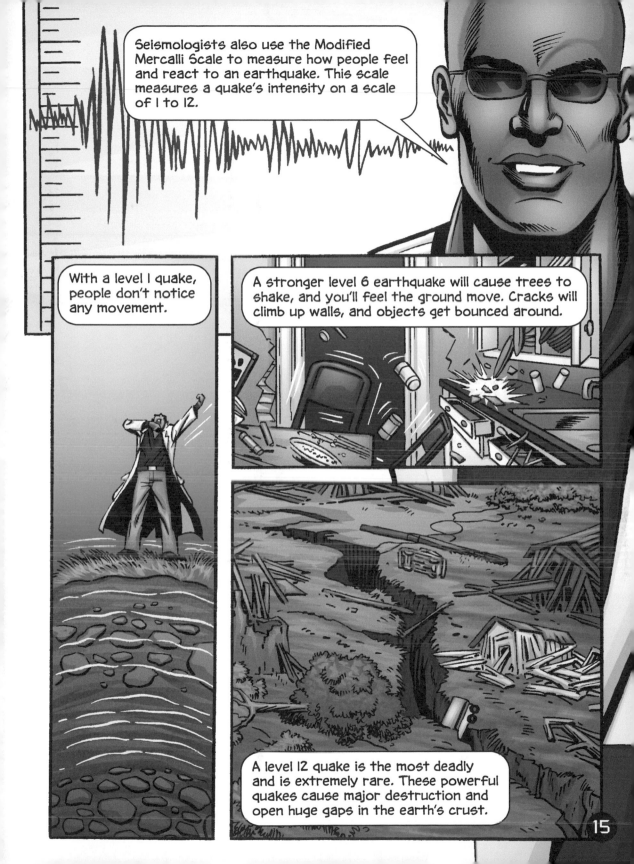

Seismologists also use the Modified Mercalli Scale to measure how people feel and react to an earthquake. This scale measures a quake's intensity on a scale of 1 to 12.

With a level 1 quake, people don't notice any movement.

A stronger level 6 earthquake will cause trees to shake, and you'll feel the ground move. Cracks will climb up walls, and objects get bounced around.

A level 12 quake is the most deadly and is extremely rare. These powerful quakes cause major destruction and open huge gaps in the earth's crust.

15

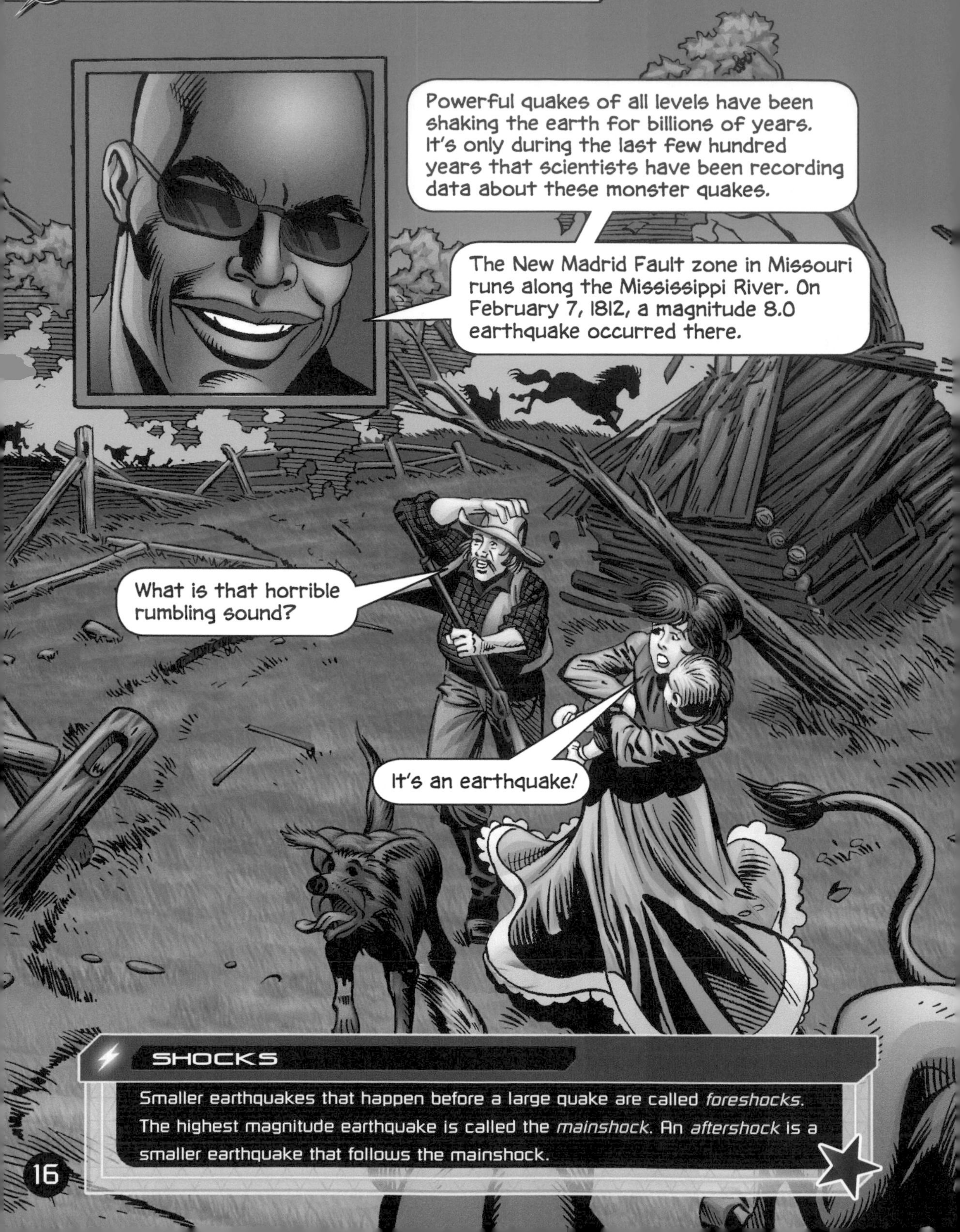
Powerful quakes of all levels have been shaking the earth for billions of years. It's only during the last few hundred years that scientists have been recording data about these monster quakes.
The New Madrid Fault zone in Missouri runs along the Mississippi River. On February 7, 1812, a magnitude 8.0 earthquake occurred there.
What is that horrible rumbling sound?
It's an earthquake!

SHOCKS

Smaller earthquakes that happen before a large quake are called *foreshocks*. The highest magnitude earthquake is called the *mainshock*. An *aftershock* is a smaller earthquake that follows the mainshock.

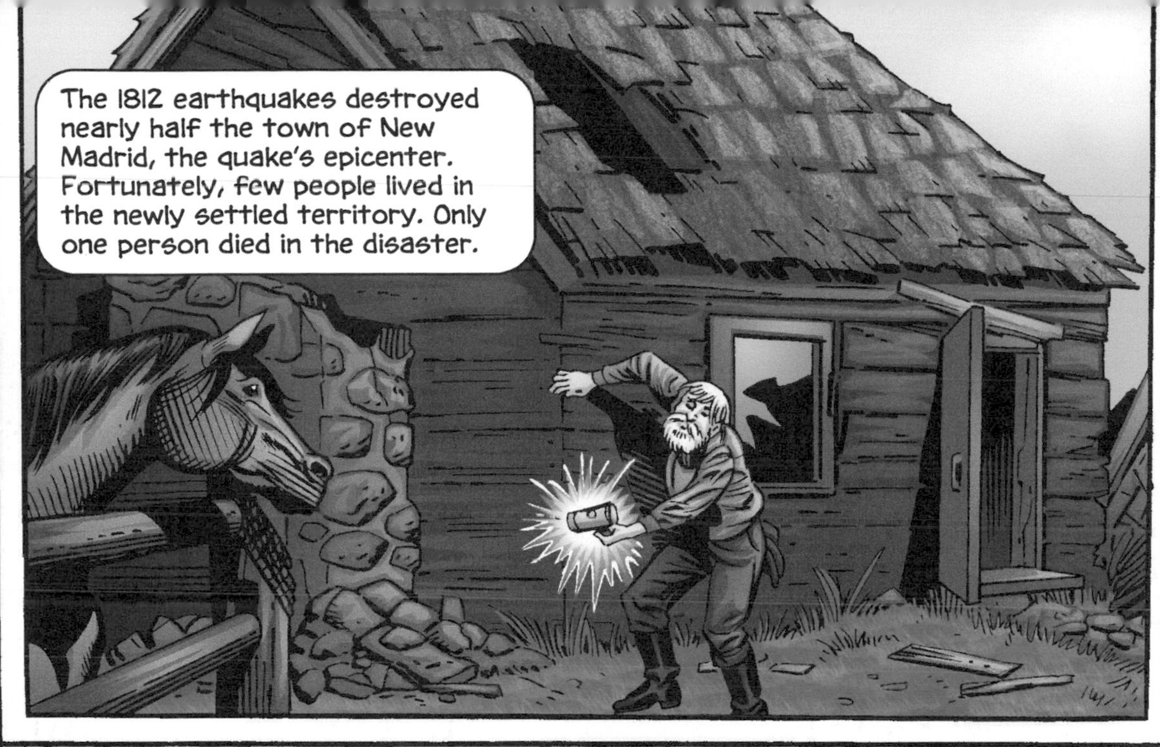
The 1812 earthquakes destroyed nearly half the town of New Madrid, the quake's epicenter. Fortunately, few people lived in the newly settled territory. Only one person died in the disaster.

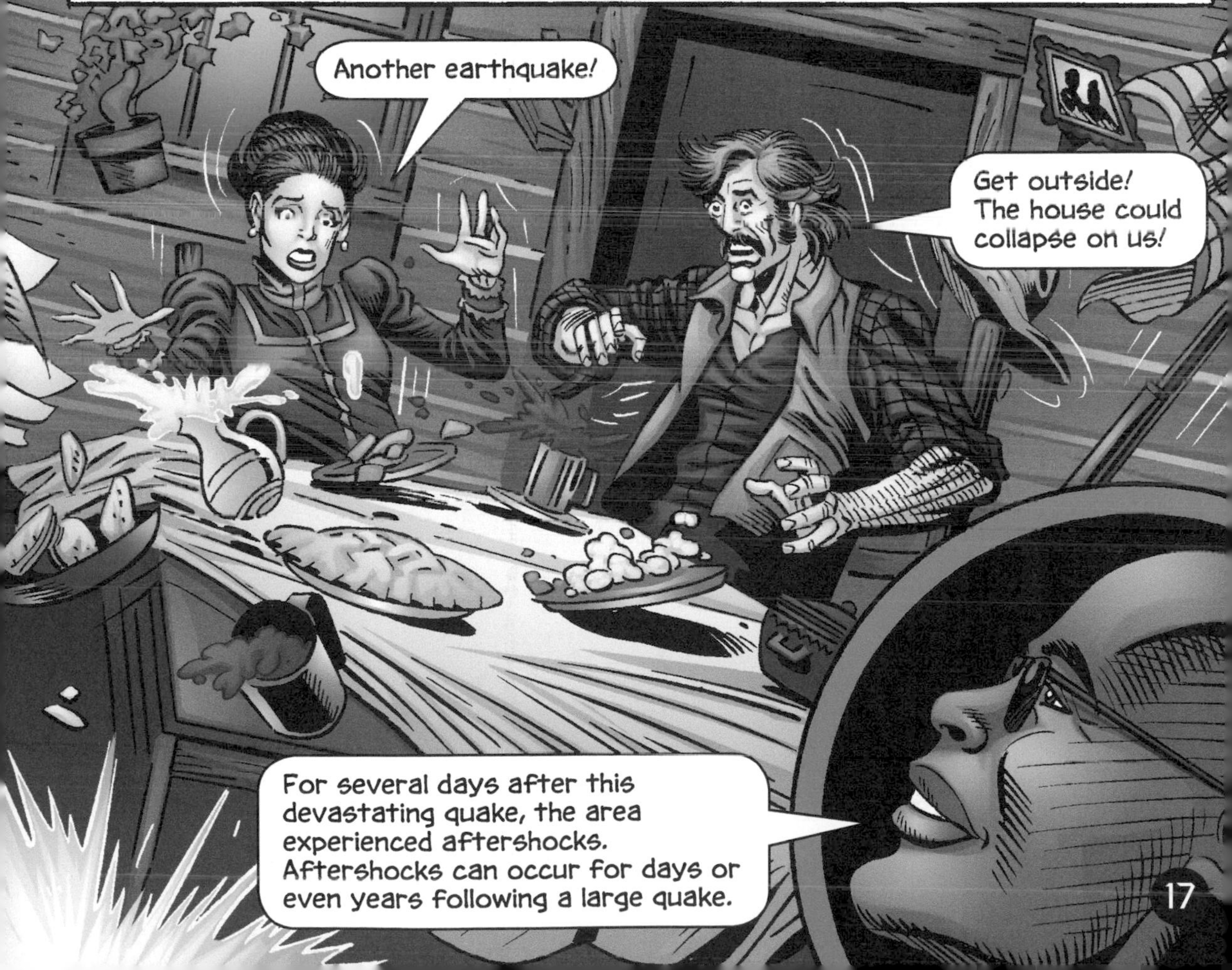
Another earthquake!
Get outside! The house could collapse on us!
For several days after this devastating quake, the area experienced aftershocks. Aftershocks can occur for days or even years following a large quake.

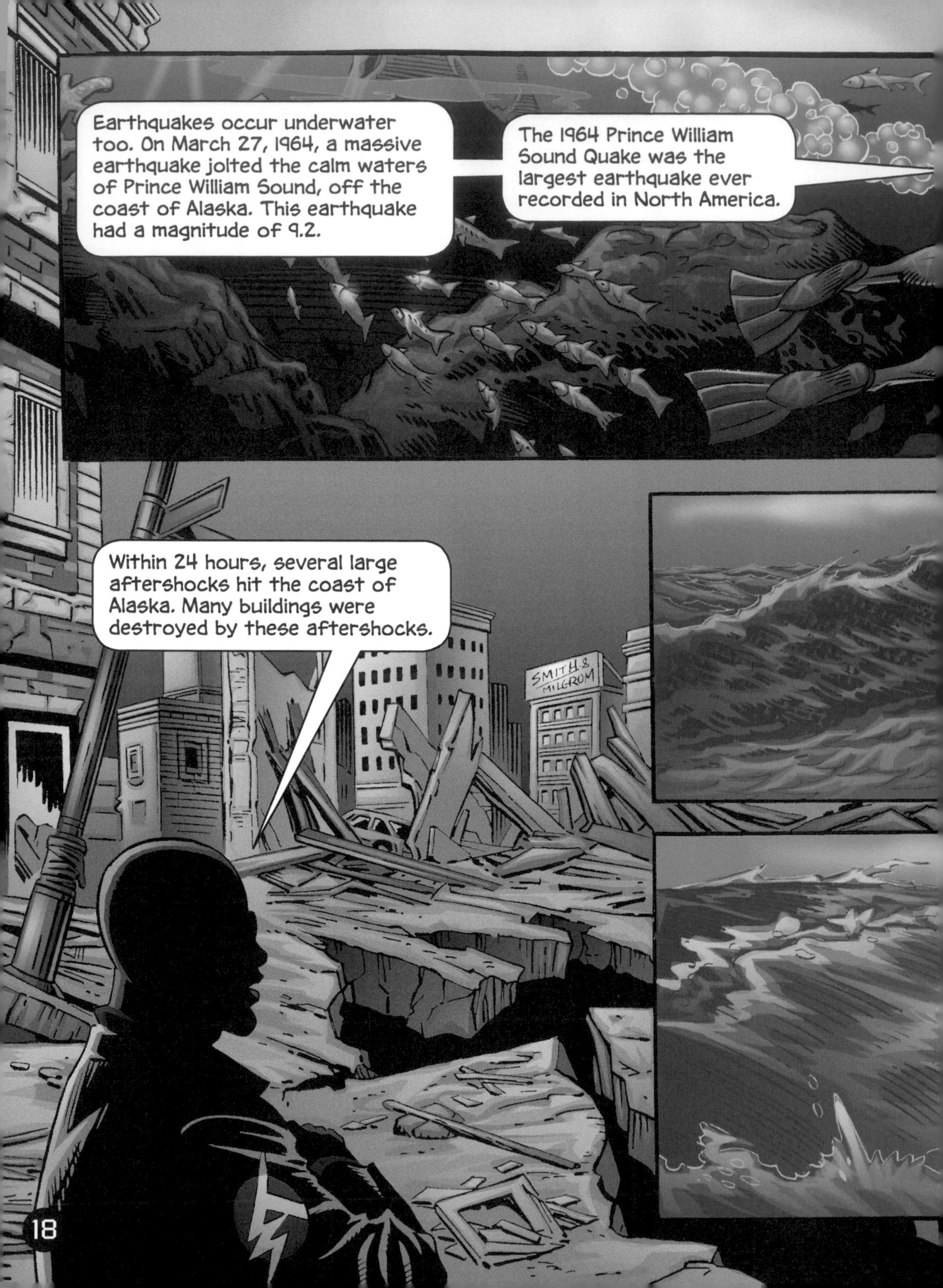
Earthquakes occur underwater too. On March 27, 1964, a massive earthquake jolted the calm waters of Prince William Sound, off the coast of Alaska. This earthquake had a magnitude of 9.2.
The 1964 Prince William Sound Quake was the largest earthquake ever recorded in North America.
Within 24 hours, several large aftershocks hit the coast of Alaska. Many buildings were destroyed by these aftershocks.
SMITH & MILGROM

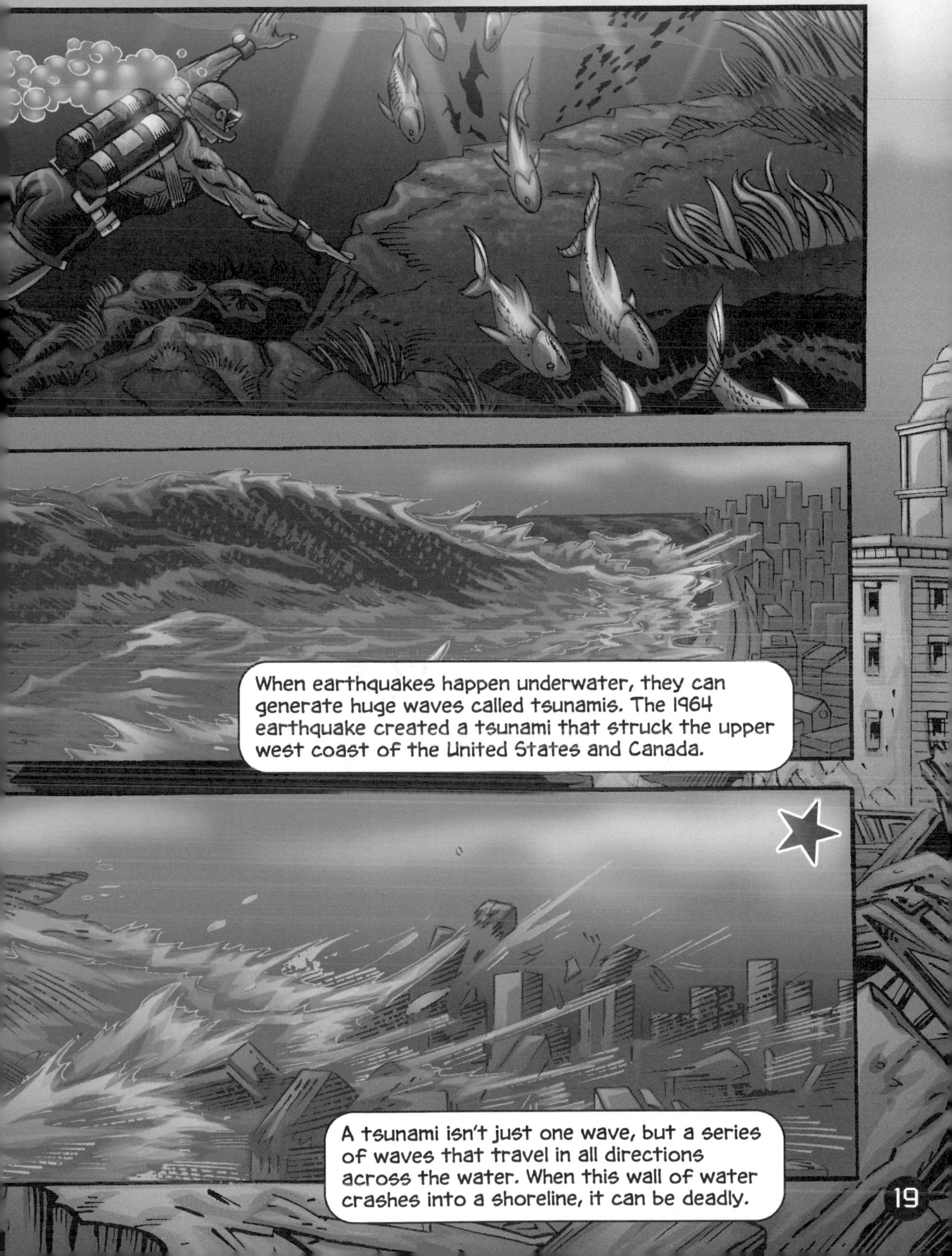
When earthquakes happen underwater, they can generate huge waves called tsunamis. The 1964 earthquake created a tsunami that struck the upper west coast of the United States and Canada.
A tsunami isn't just one wave, but a series of waves that travel in all directions across the water. When this wall of water crashes into a shoreline, it can be deadly.

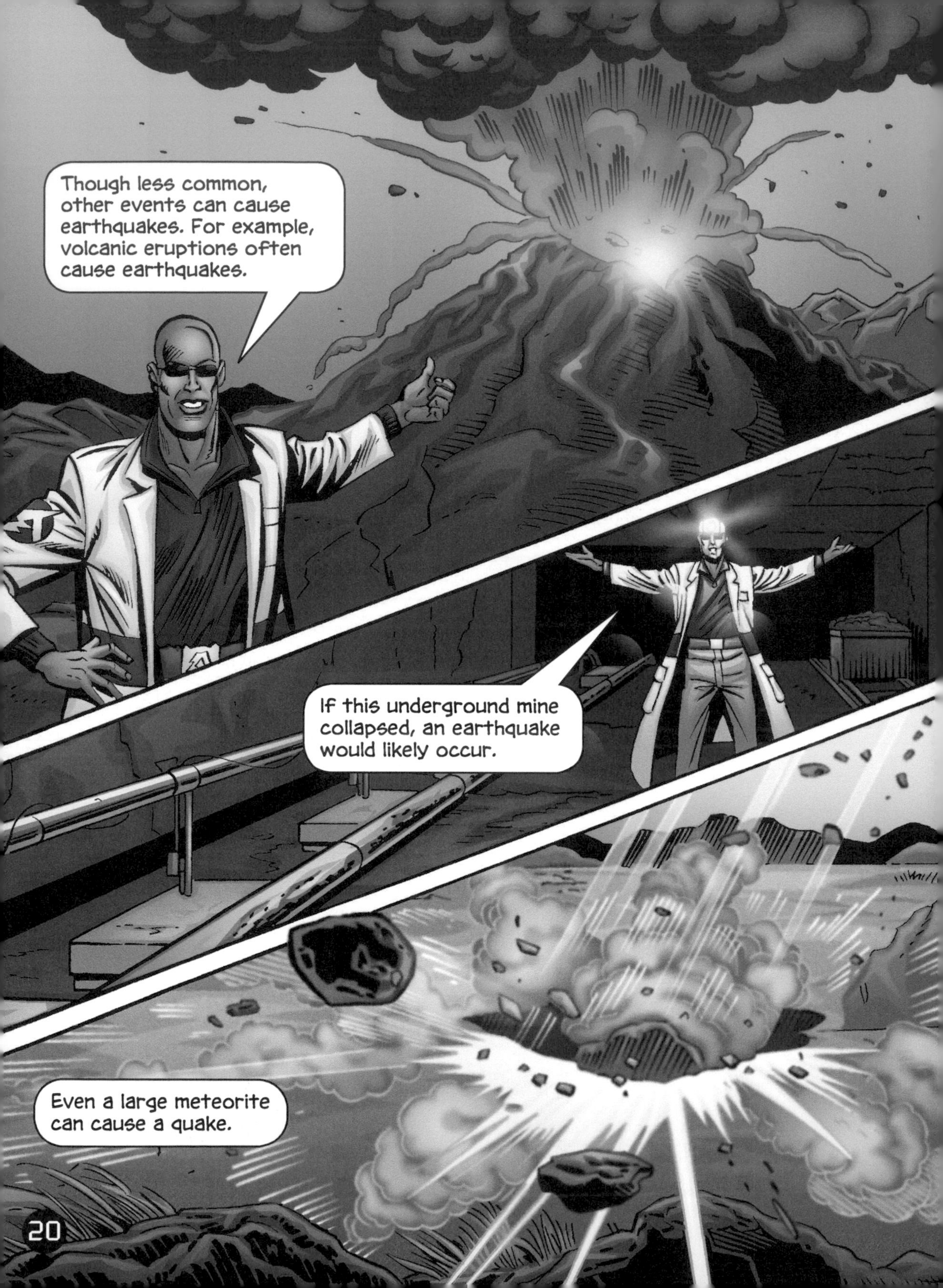
Though less common, other events can cause earthquakes. For example, volcanic eruptions often cause earthquakes.
If this underground mine collapsed, an earthquake would likely occur.
Even a large meteorite can cause a quake.

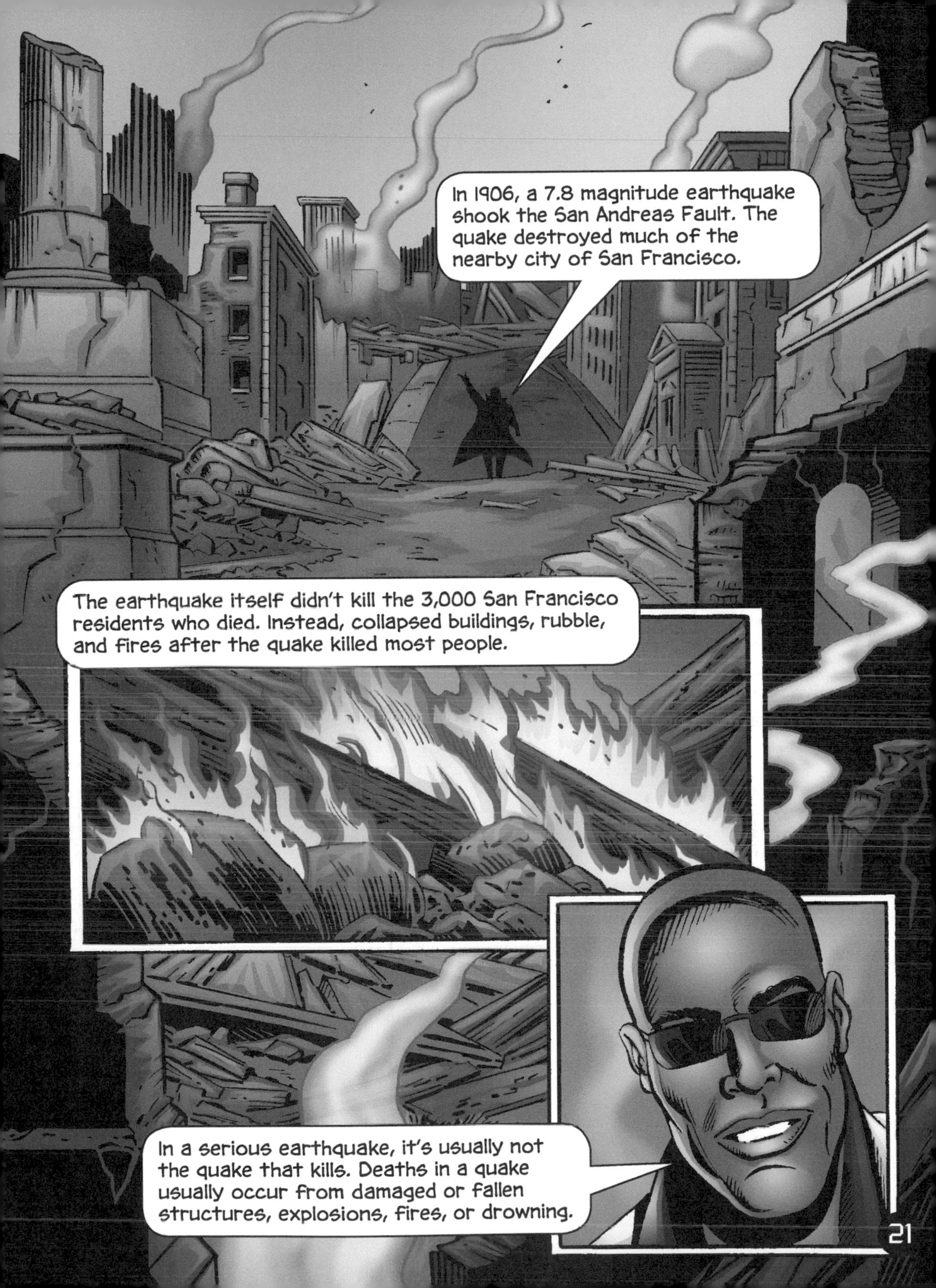
In 1906, a 7.8 magnitude earthquake shook the San Andreas Fault. The quake destroyed much of the nearby city of San Francisco.
The earthquake itself didn't kill the 3,000 San Francisco residents who died. Instead, collapsed buildings, rubble, and fires after the quake killed most people.
In a serious earthquake, it's usually not the quake that kills. Deaths in a quake usually occur from damaged or fallen structures, explosions, fires, or drowning.

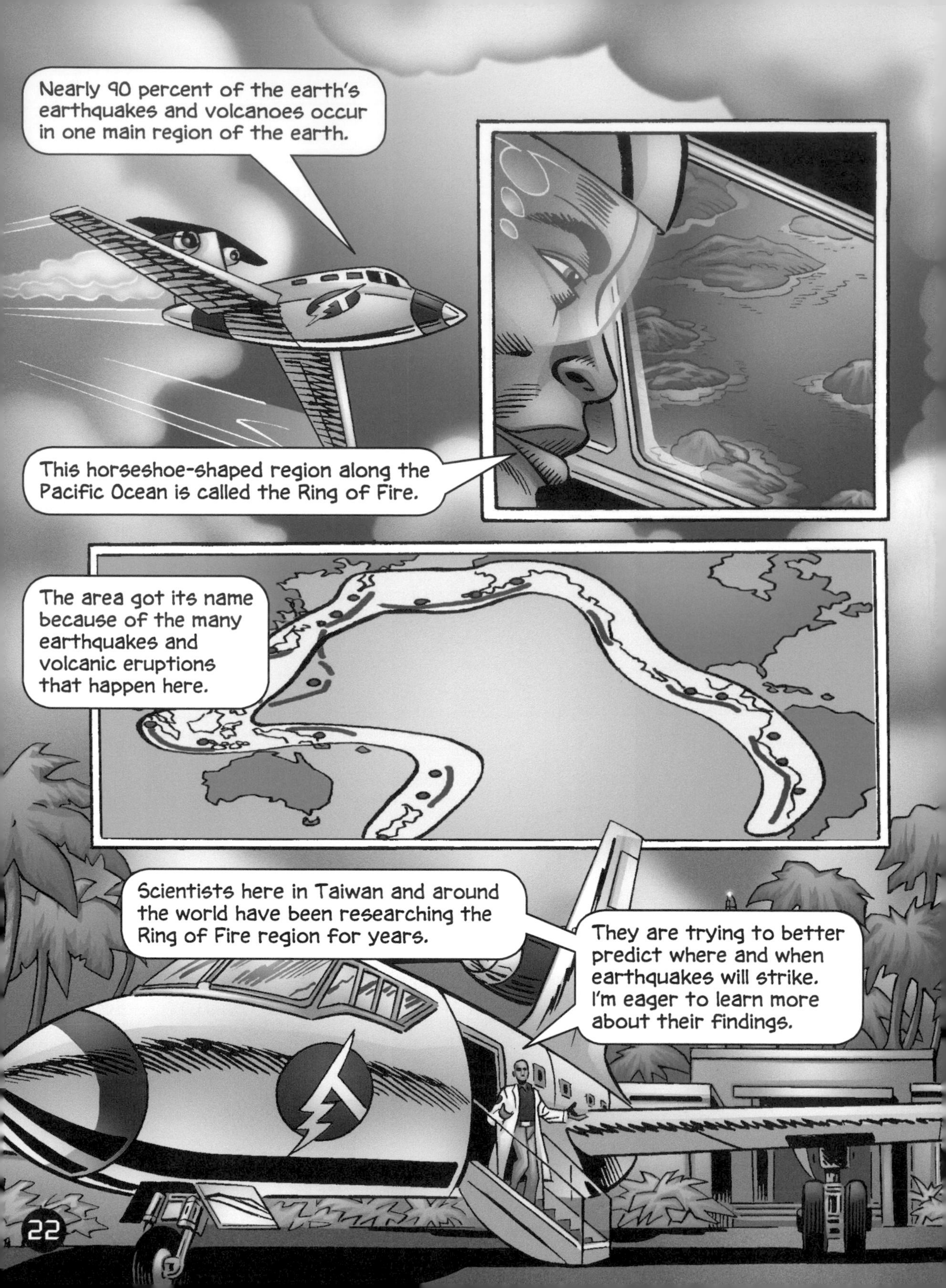

Nearly 90 percent of the earth's earthquakes and volcanoes occur in one main region of the earth.
This horseshoe-shaped region along the Pacific Ocean is called the Ring of Fire.
The area got its name because of the many earthquakes and volcanic eruptions that happen here.
Scientists here in Taiwan and around the world have been researching the Ring of Fire region for years.
They are trying to better predict where and when earthquakes will strike. I'm eager to learn more about their findings.

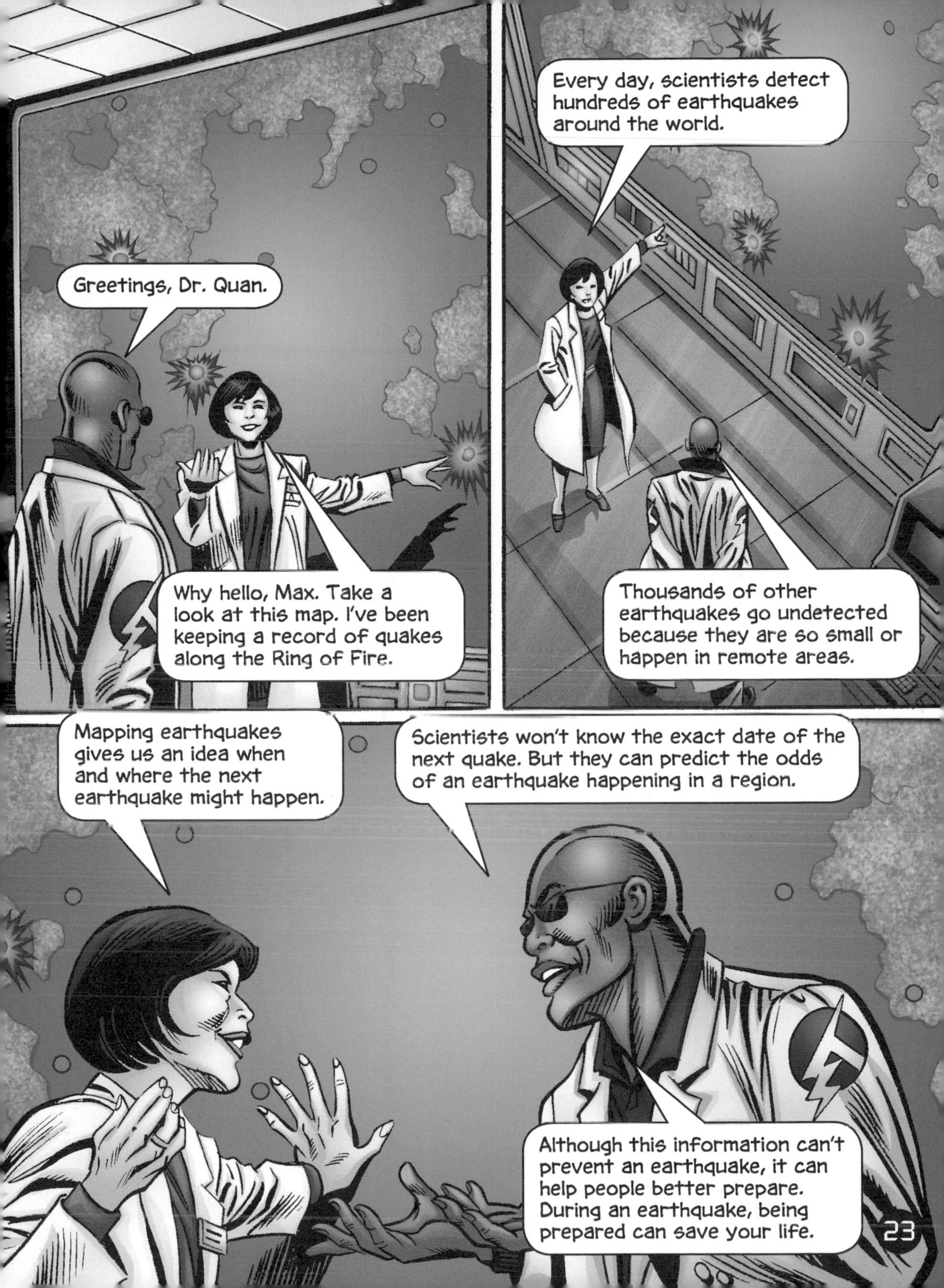
Greetings, Dr. Quan.
Why hello, Max. Take a look at this map. I've been keeping a record of quakes along the Ring of Fire.
Every day, scientists detect hundreds of earthquakes around the world.
Thousands of other earthquakes go undetected because they are so small or happen in remote areas.
Mapping earthquakes gives us an idea when and where the next earthquake might happen.
Scientists won't know the exact date of the next quake. But they can predict the odds of an earthquake happening in a region.
Although this information can't prevent an earthquake, it can help people better prepare. During an earthquake, being prepared can save your life.

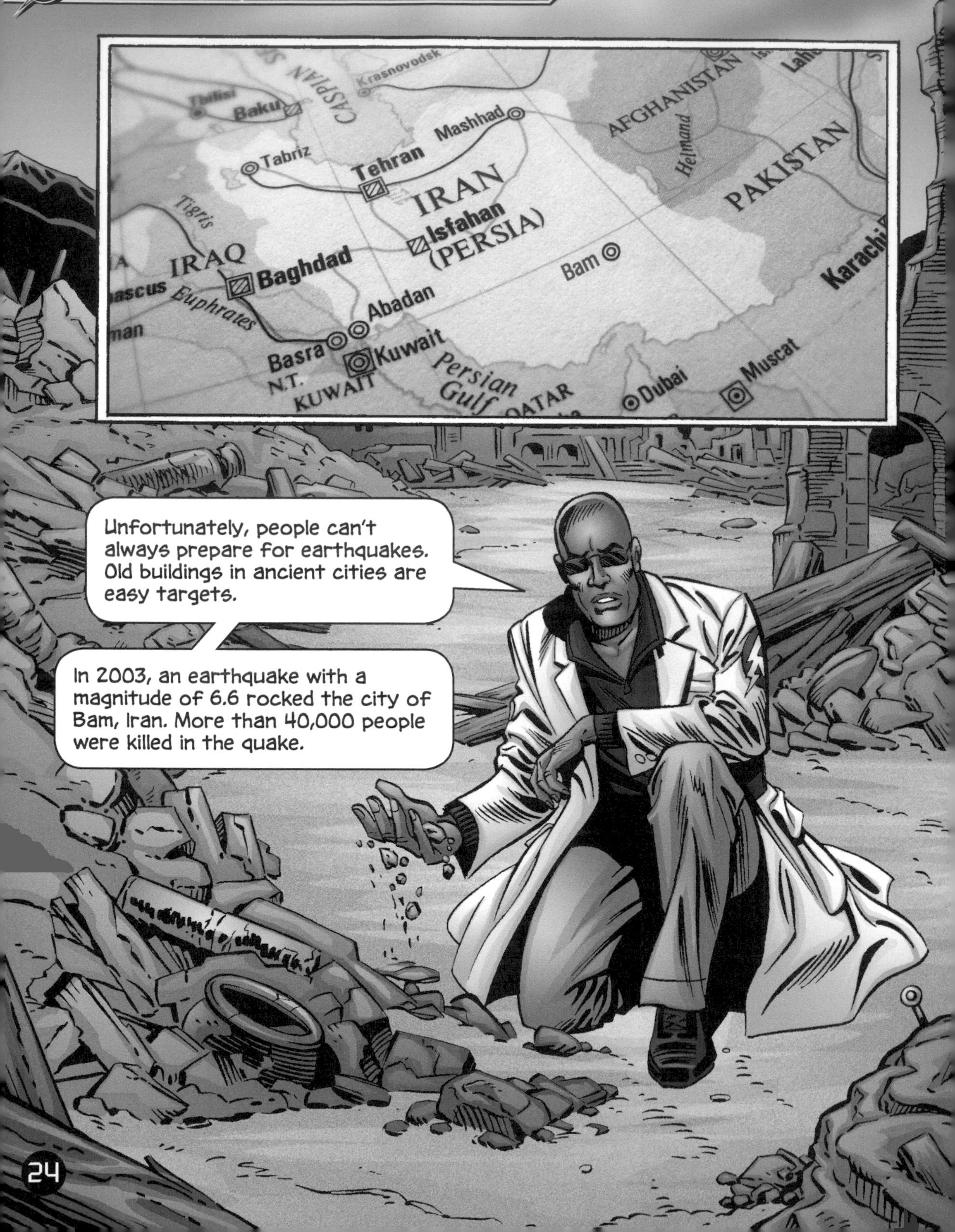
Krasnovodsk
Tbilisi
Baku
CASPIAN SEA
Mashhad
AFGHANISTAN
Helmand
PAKISTAN
Tabriz
Tehran
IRAN
Isfahan
(PERSIA)
Tigris
IRAQ
Baghdad
Bam
Karachi
Buphrates
Abadan
Basra
Kuwait
N.T.
KUWAIT
Persian Gulf
QATAR
Dubai
Muscat
Unfortunately, people can't always prepare for earthquakes. Old buildings in ancient cities are easy targets.
In 2003, an earthquake with a magnitude of 6.6 rocked the city of Bam, Iran. More than 40,000 people were killed in the quake.

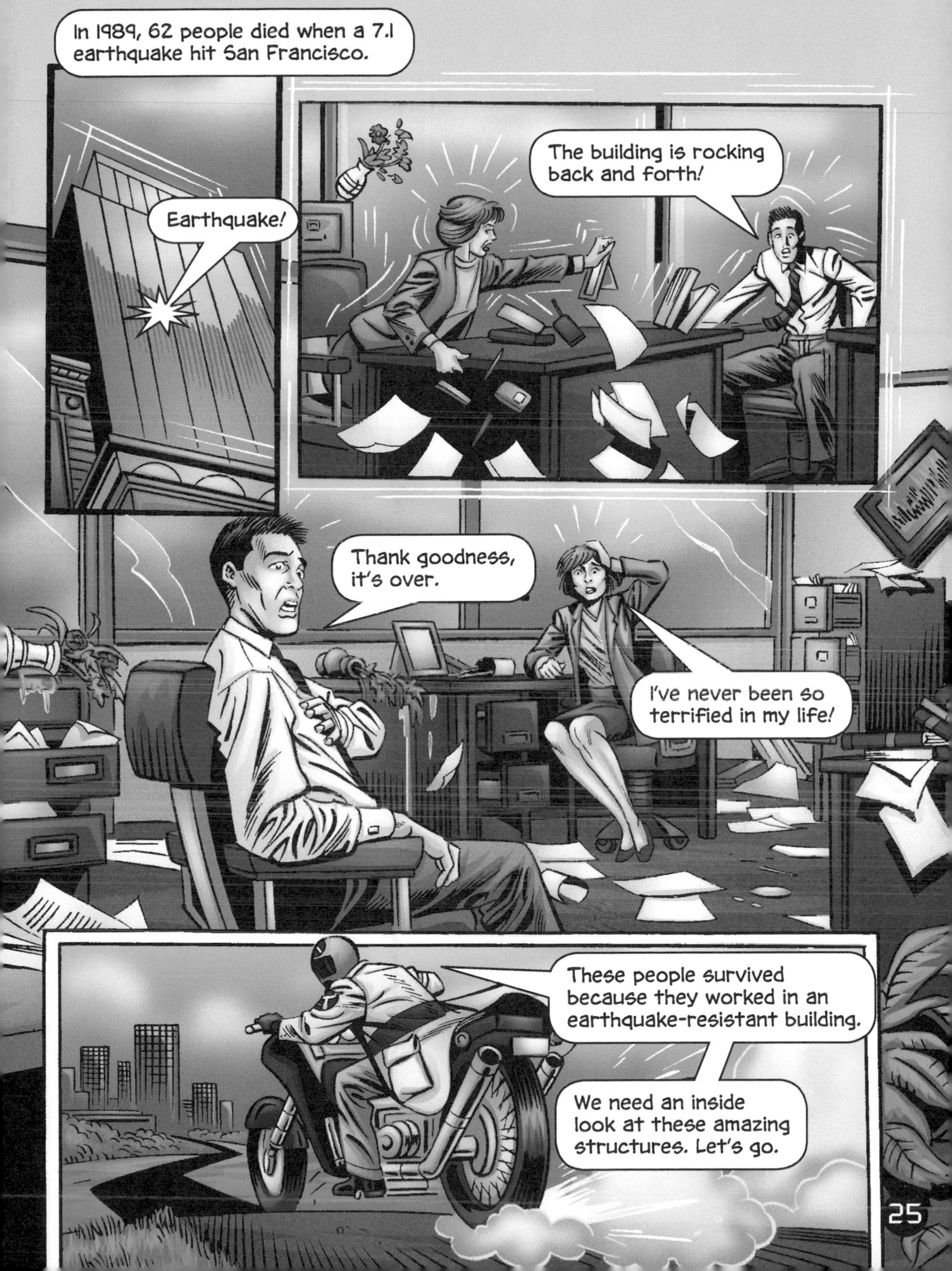
In 1989, 62 people died when a 7.1 earthquake hit San Francisco.
Earthquake!
The building is rocking back and forth!
Thank goodness, it's over.
I've never been so terrified in my life!
These people survived because they worked in an earthquake-resistant building.
We need an inside look at these amazing structures. Let's go.

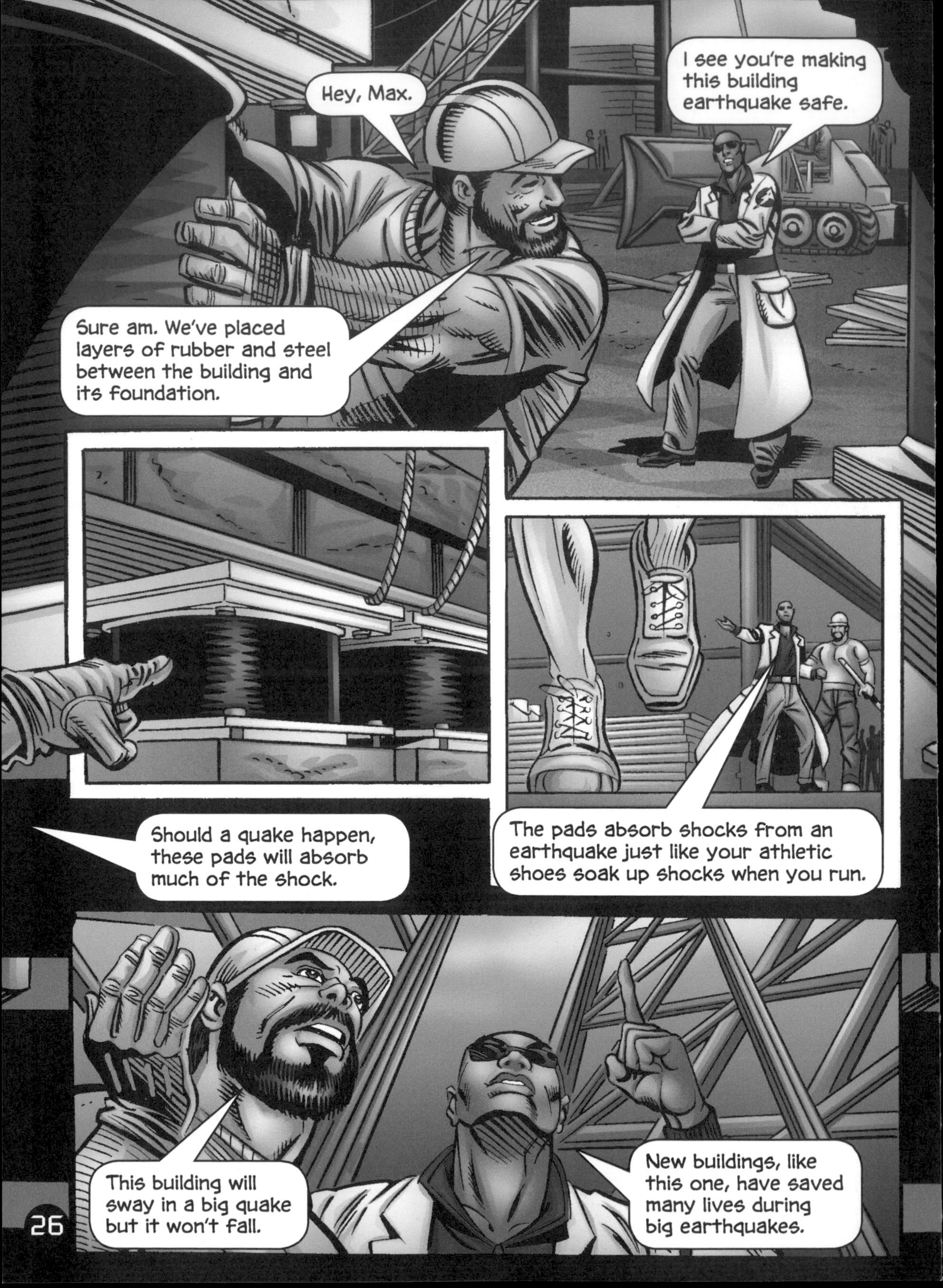
Hey, Max.
I see you're making this building earthquake safe.
Sure am. We've placed layers of rubber and steel between the building and its foundation.
Should a quake happen, these pads will absorb much of the shock.
The pads absorb shocks from an earthquake just like your athletic shoes soak up shocks when you run.
This building will sway in a big quake but it won't fall.
New buildings, like this one, have saved many lives during big earthquakes.

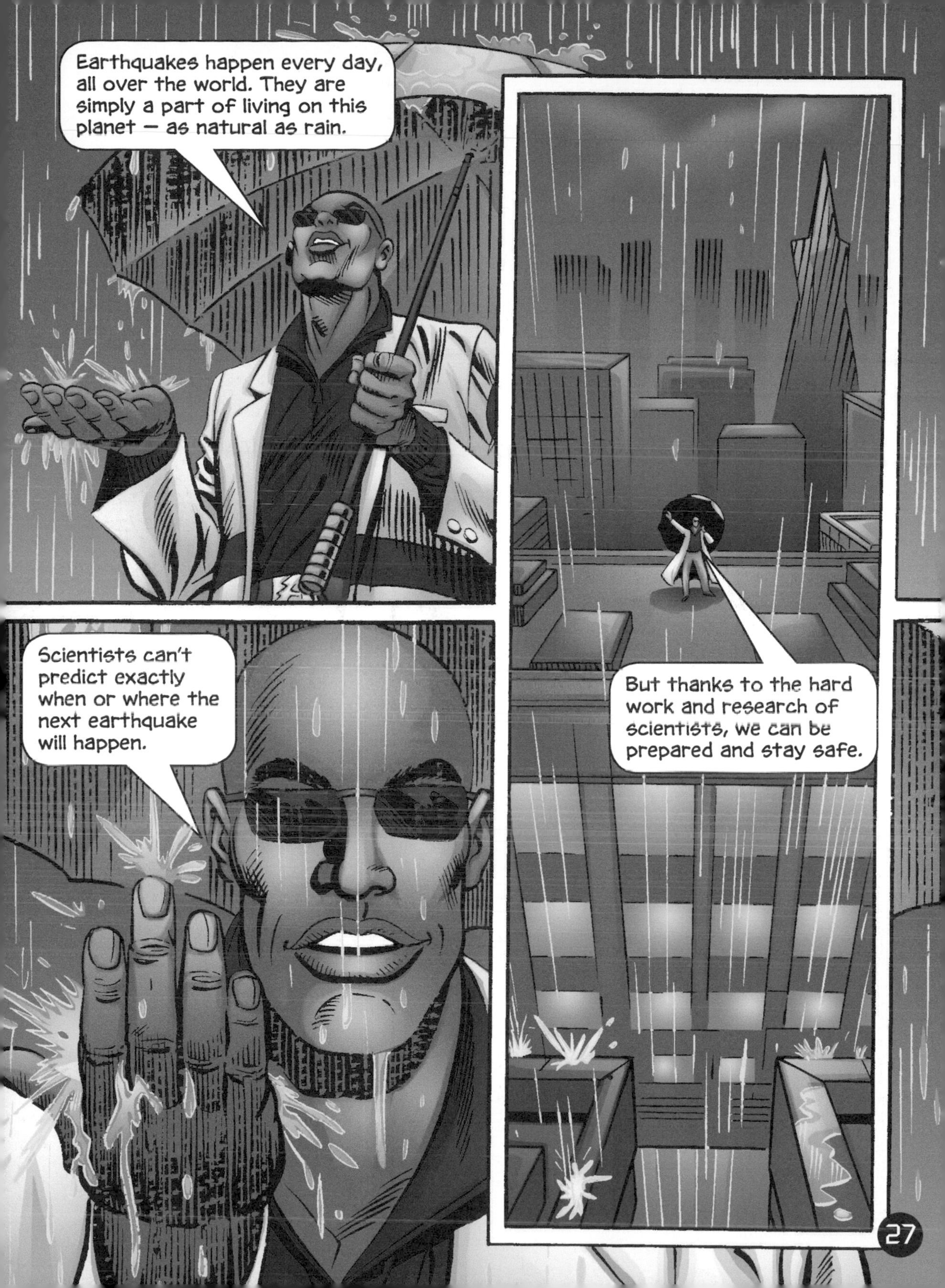
Earthquakes happen every day, all over the world. They are simply a part of living on this planet — as natural as rain.
Scientists can't predict exactly when or where the next earthquake will happen.
But thanks to the hard work and research of scientists, we can be prepared and stay safe.

MORE ABOUT EARTHQUAKES

About 500,000 earthquakes are detected by seismologists in the world each year. Of these earthquakes, only about 100,000 can be felt. Only about 100 earthquakes each year cause damage.

Scientists have learned that the crustal plate of India collided with the crust of Asia to form the Himalaya Mountains. Scientists believe these mountains are still pushing together and slowly rising.

The largest earthquake of the 20th century occurred in Chile on May 22, 1960. This quake registered 9.5 on the Richter scale. The greatest number of people killed in one earthquake was in China in 1556. The quake killed about 830,000 people.

Tsunami waves can be far-reaching and deadly. Waves from the 1964 Alaska earthquake struck many towns in the Prince William Sound area of Alaska and along the Gulf of Alaska. These waves killed 21 people in Alaska.

Caused by earthquakes, volcanic eruptions, or landslides, tsunamis can travel at speeds up to 600 miles (966 kilometers) per hour.

Researchers in Buffalo, New York, discovered that rubber pads placed under earthquake-resistant buildings can cut the force of a quake by 25 percent.

Geologist A. C. Lawson named the San Andreas Fault in 1895. He named it after the San Andreas Lake, located on the fault, about 20 miles (32 km) south of San Francisco.

Plate movement along the San Andreas Fault created many mountainous areas. Scientists have studied the Transverse Range segment the most.

Southern California has about 10,000 earthquakes each year. North Dakota and Florida have had the fewest number of earthquakes in the United States.

EARTH-POUNDING P-WAVES

Make your own earthquake wave box to see P-waves in action!

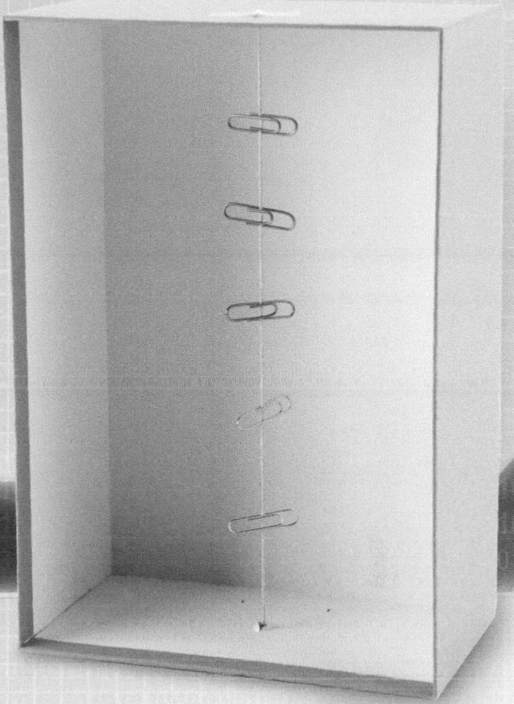

WHAT YOU NEED:

- shoebox
- pencil
- scissors
- string
- tape
- 5 paper clips
- table

WHAT YOU DO:

1. Remove the lid from the shoebox.
2. Use a pencil to carefully punch a hole in the center of the box's short sides.
3. Cut a length of string that is about 2 inches (5 cm) longer than the shoebox.
4. Thread the string through the holes punched in step 2. Pull the string taut and tape the ends to the outsides of the box.
5. Stand the box up the long way on a table. Fasten the paper clips to the string, spacing them out evenly.
6. Ball your hand into a fist and pound it on the table. Watch the paper clips vibrate as P-waves travel from the table, through the box, and into the string.
7. Experiment with pounding on the table harder and softer. Observe the differences in the way the paper clips move on the string as you change the strength of your "earthquake."

DISCUSSION QUESTIONS

1. Most earthquakes occur along faults in earth's crust. What are the main types of faults and how does each one move?

2. Scientists measure earthquakes by their magnitude and intensity. What is the difference between them? What scales are used to measure each?

3. What is the Ring of Fire? Why is this area important to scientists who study volcanoes and earthquakes?

4. Imagine you are designing an earthquake-resistant building. What types of features would your building have and how would they keep people safe during an earthquake?

WRITING PROMPTS

1. Based on the illustration on page 6, draw your own cross-section diagram of the earth's layers. Label the layers and write a short caption describing each one.

2. Not all earthquakes occur along earth's faults. Make a list of other events that can cause earthquakes. Then pick one and write a short paragraph explaining how it causes the earth to shake.

3. Imagine you just experienced an earthquake that caused trees to shake, cracks to climb up the walls, and books to fall off shelves. Write a short newspaper report that describes the event and lists the earthquake's level on the Modified Mercalli Scale.

4. This book highlights several major earthquakes in history. Pick one and do additional research about it online. Then write a fictional first-hand account of what it was like to live through the quake.

TAKE A QUIZ!

GLOSSARY

continental drift (KON-tuh-nuhn-tuhl DRIFT)—the slow movement of the earth's continents

core (KOR)—the inner part of earth that is made of solid and molten metal

crust (KRUHST)—the outer layer of earth; the crust is made of lighter-weight rocks

detect (di-TEKT)—to notice or discover something

epicenter (EP-uh-sent-ur)—the point on the earth's surface directly above the place where an earthquake occurs

fault (FAWLT)—a crack in earth's crust where two plates meet

fracture (FRAK-chur)—a break or crack in something

magnitude (MAG-nuh-tood)—a measure of the amount of energy released by an earthquake

mantle (MAN-tuhl)—the layer of hot, dense rock that surrounds earth's core

plate (PLAYT)—a large sheet of rock that is a piece of earth's crust

predict (pri-DIKT)—to say what you think will happen in the future

rupture (RUHP-chur)—to break open or to burst

seismic (SIZE-mik)—something that is caused by or related to an earthquake

seismogram (SIZE-muh-grahm)—the written record of an earthquake

tsunami (tsoo-NAH-mee)—a large, destructive wave caused by an underwater earthquake

volcanic eruption (vol-KAN-ik e-RUHPT-shuhn)—the action of throwing out rock, hot ash, or lava with great force

READ MORE

Elkins, Elizabeth. *Investigating Earthquakes.* Investigating Natural Disasters. North Mankato, Minn.: Capstone Press, 2017.

Farndon, John. *Extreme Earthquakes and Tsunamis.* When Nature Attacks. Minneapolis: Hungry Tomato, 2018.

Rivera, Andrea. *Earthquakes.* Zoom in on Natural Disasters. Minneapolis: Abdo Zoom, 2018.

Shea, Therese M. *Rocked by Earthquakes.* How People Survive. New York: PowerKids Press, 2018.

INTERNET SITES

Use Facthound to find Internet sites related to this book.

Visit *www.facthound.com*

Just type in 9781543558715 and go!

 Check out projects, games and lots more at
www.capstonekids.com

INDEX

aftershocks, 16, 17, 18
asthenosphere, 7

Bam, Iran, 24
buildings, 21, 24, 25, 26, 28

continents, 9

earth's layers
   crust, 6, 7, 8, 10, 11, 15
   inner core, 6
   mantle, 6, 7
   outer core, 6
earthquakes
   causes, 6, 8, 20
   damage, 4–5, 15, 18, 21
   deaths from, 17, 21, 24, 25, 28
   prediction of, 22–23, 27
   preparing for, 23, 26, 27

epicenter, 12, 17

faults, 10–11
   normal, 10
   reverse, 10
   strike-slip, 10
   thrust, 10
focus, 12
foreshock, 16

hypocenter, 12

intensity, 14, 15

magnitude, 14, 16, 18, 21, 24
mainshock, 16
Modified Mercalli Scale, 15
Mount Everest, 9
mountains, 9, 28

New Madrid Fault Zone, 16

Palmdale, California, 11
Prince William Sound, Alaska, 18–19

Richter scale, 14, 28
Ring of Fire, 22–23

San Andreas Fault, 11, 21, 28
San Francisco, 21, 25, 28
seismic waves, 11, 12, 13
   primary waves, 12
   secondary waves, 13
seismogram, 14
seismologists, 13, 14, 15, 28

tectonic plates, 7, 8, 9, 28
tsunamis, 19, 28

volcanoes, 20, 22